Samuel French Acting Edition

The Old One-Two
A Play in One Act

by A.R. Gurney Jr.

Copyright © 1971 by A.R. Gurney Jr.
All Rights Reserved

THE OLD ONE-TWO is fully protected under the copyright laws of the United States of America, the British Commonwealth, including Canada, and all other countries of the Copyright Union. All rights, including professional and amateur stage productions, recitation, lecturing, public reading, motion picture, radio broadcasting, television and the rights of translation into foreign languages are strictly reserved.

ISBN 978-0-573-62370-7

www.SamuelFrench.com
www.SamuelFrench.co.uk

For Production Enquiries

United States and Canada
Info@SamuelFrench.com
1-866-598-8449

United Kingdom and Europe
Plays@SamuelFrench.co.uk
020-7255-4302

Each title is subject to availability from Samuel French, depending upon country of performance. Please be aware that *THE OLD ONE-TWO* may not be licensed by Samuel French in your territory. Professional and amateur producers should contact the nearest Samuel French office or licensing partner to verify availability.

CAUTION: Professional and amateur producers are hereby warned that *THE OLD ONE-TWO* is subject to a licensing fee. Publication of this play(s) does not imply availability for performance. Both amateurs and professionals considering a production are strongly advised to apply to Samuel French before starting rehearsals, advertising, or booking a theatre. A licensing fee must be paid whether the title(s) is presented for charity or gain and whether or not admission is charged. Professional/Stock licensing fees are quoted upon application to Samuel French.

No one shall make any changes in this title(s) for the purpose of production. No part of this book may be reproduced, stored in a retrieval system, or transmitted in any form, by any means, now known or yet to be invented, including mechanical, electronic, photocopying, recording, videotaping, or otherwise, without the prior written permission of the publisher. No one shall upload this title(s), or part of this title(s), to any social media websites.

For all enquiries regarding motion picture, television, and other media rights, please contact Samuel French.

Please refer to page 42 for further copyright information.

PLOT SUMMARY

A Professor of Classics at an American university becomes obsessed with a girl student, who challenges the relevance of his course and finally leads him into an overnight affair. Meanwhile, the Dean of the department, joining her in the attempt to bring the curriculum up to date, has become involved in a sly relationship with the Professor's mysterious wife. The play is saved from a tragic ending by a sudden, surprising discovery.

CAST

AUGUSTUS HOLDER, *Professor of Classics at an American university.*

SUSAN GREEN, *a student.*

THE DEAN

SET

Four playing areas:

1. An old oaken lectern, facing out, from which PROFESSOR HOLDER addresses his class.
2. PROFESSOR HOLDER'S office. A cluttered desk with books, notes, papers. A Greek bust on it. A telephone. A picture of the Parthenon behind. Two chairs, one behind the desk, one in front.
3. The DEAN'S office. A metal desk with push-button telephones, a dictaphone, an electric typewriter. Modern furniture, an abstract painting on the wall.
4. SUSAN GREEN'S room in a dormitory. A wooden chair and institutional desk. Paperback books and records scattered around. Posters about peace and ecology on the wall. A wall dorm-line telephone.

The play takes place during the Fall of the current academic year.

The Old One-Two

As the houselights dim, PROFESSOR HOLDER *comes out and goes to the lectern. He carries an old battered leather briefcase and a black umbrella. He wears an old-fashioned, rumpled dark suit, white shirt, dark tie. He is in his 50's, graying, and has an Old World charm about him. He leans his umbrella carefully against the lectern, places his briefcase on the lectern, and carefully removes a couple of books and lecture notes, arranging them on the lectern. He puts his briefcase neatly next to his umbrella. He puts on a pair of steel-rimmed glasses, surveys his notes, takes off the glasses, surveys the audience, and finally begins. He speaks with a slight foreign accent.*

HOLDER. (*To audience.*) Good morning . . . This course is entitled Introduction to Humanities. Colon. The Classical Experience. (*A wry smile.*) It is known to students—affectionately, I hope—as the Old One-Two. (*Pause.*) Old, because I have taught it in this university for a great many years. (*Pause.*) One-Two because I teach it both semesters. In that way, those of you who fail it in the fall can repeat it in the spring. (*Pause.*) I should only add that this is a required course for all students in the liberal arts. Over the years, it has been attacked, occupied, ravaged, and abused. But it has stood. It stands. It will stand. Mutilated, but beautiful. Like the Parthenon. (*A pretty* GIRL, *in casual clothes, carrying books and papers, gets up from her seat in one of the rear rows and edges her way out to the Center aisle. She may ad-lib "Excuse me . . . Sorry. . . ."* HOLDER *sees her, over the top of his glasses; he watches her patiently and finally speaks.*) Just a minute, please. (*The* GIRL *continues toward the door.*) I said just a minute, please. (*The* GIRL *stops.*) What's the difficulty, please?

GIRL. I'm in the wrong course.

HOLDER. You are in the right course.

GIRL. No, I mean wrong for me.

HOLDER. How do you know?

GIRL. How do I *know?*

HOLDER. (*Patiently.*) How do you know this course is wrong for you.

GIRL. Oh. Well, you see I'm interested in Urban Studies.

HOLDER. Good. Here you will study Athens and Rome. Sit down, please.

GIRL. Oh no. I mean contemporary urban problems. (*Pause. He waits.*) Like traffic patterns . . . (*He still waits.*) And slums . . .

HOLDER. You want to study traffic? You want to study slums?

GIRL. Exactly.

HOLDER. Oh dear. Well. Study what you want. But first you must have the Classical Experience.

GIRL. But I don't want the Classical Experience.

HOLDER. That's not the point. The gods of this university, in their infinite wisdom, long ago decreed that you cannot know yourself until you know your tradition. You cannot study traffic and slums until you study Homer and Sophocles. You cannot be taken seriously as an educated person—until you have taken me. (*Pause.*)

GIRL. (*Suddenly defiant.*) I'll see the Dean.

HOLDER. He'll send you back.

GIRL. The *new* Dean?

HOLDER. Any Dean.

GIRL. I'll take a substitute.

HOLDER. There are no substitutes.

GIRL. I'll petition, I'll appeal.

HOLDER. (*Shaking his head.*) No petition, no appeal.

GIRL. Why that's absolutely, totally unfair!
HOLDER. Ah hah! There! You see what you've learned? Already you've arrived at a primitive conception of Greek tragedy! Think about that. And sit down.
GIRL. No, I won't. I won't think about that. And I won't sit down, either. And I won't study the Greeks. I'm going to find a way out of the Old One-Two! (*She walks out. We hear a door slam in the rear.* HOLDER *sighs, and speaks to the audience.*)
HOLDER. During the term, you will read a number of Greek plays. And in them, you will discover several splendid young heroines. Antigone, Polyxena, Iphigenia . . . (*He loves these words.*) . . . all these maidens will you meet. And you will see them stand up bravely to authority. And go to their death for it, singing fine, pure, triumphant songs. And you will realize that there is a great tradition of personal protest in our culture. And you will recall this recent exhibition, and you will see it as a poor, sad parody of that tradition. And you will shudder with shame. (*He returns to his notes, is now all business.*) Your first paper, on Homer, of at least two thousand words, will be due a week from Monday. I personally will read and grade your work. Try hard! Like the Greeks we study, I believe in fate, struggle, honor, and sudden death. Plan your weekends accordingly. (*He holds up a battered, leathery volume, stuffed with notes.*) Now Homer. *The Odyssey.* I translate from the Greek. (*He reads, carefully translating.*) "Sing inside of me, Muse, and through *me only* let the story be told . . ."

(*The lights fade out on* HOLDER *and the lectern; they fade up on the* DEAN, *in his office. He is in his early thirties, modishly dressed, and at this point is answering an intercom in his office.*)

DEAN. O.K. Send her in. (*The* GIRL *comes in.*) Hi.
SUSAN. I'm—
DEAN. Susan Green. I know. I heard all about you. I'm

the new Dean. (*He shakes her hand enthusiastically.*) Now here's what I've done. I've reserved a room for you at the student center. Big enough for a reasonably large crowd. I've scheduled it for seven-thirty. I thought that was a good time: after the meal and before the movies. My secretary will help you run off announcements on the Xerox, and then I'll dig up people to help you post them on bulletin boards around the campus. O.K.?

SUSAN. But I don't want that.

DEAN. You don't want to have a protest meeting?

SUSAN. No, I just want to get out of the course.

DEAN. Oh. Gee. I thought you were going to protest.

SUSAN. Uh uh. Not me. I'm not the type. (*Pause.*)

DEAN. (*Sitting down, sadly.*) Darn.

SUSAN. I want to change to the social sciences.

DEAN. You, too, huh? I mean we're losing half our students because of that course, and no one even wants to protest.

SUSAN. Why don't you fire him?

DEAN. Can't. He's got tenure.

SUSAN. Why don't you get rid of the course?

DEAN. Can't. There are too many old men around this place who think it's essential.

SUSAN. But the students hate it.

DEAN. They don't show it. They either get out of it, like you, or else retire to their room and write a two thousand word paper, without a whimper. God. Where is the spirit of the sixties? I'm going back to teaching Romantic poetry. There's more excitement in Wordsworth's "Daffodils" than there is in the corridors of power these days. Well many thanks, anyway, for lighting a small temporary candle in a dark Nixon world.

SUSAN. If we protested, what would you do?

DEAN. Oh I'd have an excuse to break up the course.

SUSAN. Break it up?

DEAN. Sure. Kids could choose. You could take Professor Birnhaum on Culture and Counterculture. You could take Miss Russell on Sex and Sexuality. You could take Mr. Johnson on Black Power. (*He shows her a catalogue.*)

SUSAN. Oh what fabulous courses!

DEAN. They could be. But I'll have to cancel all three of them if we continue to lose our enrollment. (*Pause.*)

SUSAN. All right. Then I *will* protest. I will call that meeting. (*The* DEAN *looks at her, goes to her, gives her a big hug.*)

DEAN. There! That's what we did in the sixties. And if you mention any of this to anyone else, I'll deny it ever happened. Now get going, baby. The Xerox is waiting. You do your part, I'll do mine, and we'll have this place swinging in six months. (*She goes out. He dials the telephone quickly, all the while humming "Hey Jude."*)

DEAN. Let me speak to the treasurer, please. (*More "Hey Jude."*) Bill? . . . It's me . . . You know that crazy fascist alumnus who wants to give money to the Old One-Two . . . Listen, I think I've got a way we can use it now. . . . Supposing Holder gets tired and wants a rest . . .

(*The lights fade on him, and fade up on* HOLDER, *who is also on the telephone.*)

HOLDER. Hello, Darling . . . I'm coming home early today. Will you meet the four o'clock bus? . . . Yes. A bad day . . . The Old One-Two . . . The usual flurry of complaints at the beginning of the term. This time, a silly young girl. I wonder if I'm getting too old to play the villain . . . Goodbye, darling. See you at four.

(HOLDER *hangs up, puts on his overcoat, grabs his briefcase, and exits as the lights dim on his office. The lights come up on the lectern.* SUSAN GREEN *comes nervously down the aisle.*)

SUSAN. (*Nervously; to audience.*) Before the bell rings, before he gets here . . . (*Glances off.*) . . . I'm supposed to say . . . for the people who couldn't make the meeting last night . . . well, we met, and took a vote, and decided not to write that first paper. Hear that, everyone? . . . It's a strike. O.K.? We're striking . . . And anyone who finks out, anyone who writes that paper, will hear about it. From me. O.K.? (*Pause; glances off again.*) And I was elected to tell him. (*Pause. She stands nervously in the aisle. Then the bell rings.* HOLDER *comes out, briefcase and all. He seems not to see her, and sets up his books and notes as usual. Finally, when he is all set, he calls out to her.*)

HOLDER. Now. Who are you?

SUSAN. You know who I am.

HOLDER. Ah so I do. Forgive me. You all look alike. The hair, the clothes . . . I'm particularly fascinated by the clothes. This yearning of upper middleclass American children for the bucolic. It's charmingly decadent. We went through it in Europe in the 18th century. The French call it "nostalgie de la boue"—longing for the gutter. You, as I recall, long for the slums.

SUSAN. (*Suddenly.*) We refuse to write the first paper. (*Pause.*)

HOLDER. Come up here, please. (*Pause.*)

SUSAN. All right. (*She starts for the stage.*)

HOLDER. I want everyone to see and hear you.

SUSAN. All right. (*She mounts the stage, stands near the edge.*)

HOLDER. (*To* SUSAN.) Now. Repeat what you said.

SUSAN. We refuse to write the first paper.

HOLDER. Who refuses?

SUSAN. We. (*Indicating audience.*) Us.

HOLDER. "We" is correct. The nominative case. The subject of the verb "refuse."

SUSAN. Well, we do.

HOLDER. The first paper.

SUSAN. Yes.

HOLDER. On Homer?

SUSAN. Yes. On Homer. We refuse to write it.

HOLDER. Why?

SUSAN. Because . . . two thousand words is too much.

HOLDER. Too much? On Homer?
SUSAN. We have other things to do.
HOLDER. Such as what?
SUSAN. Other courses. Other activities.
HOLDER. I know the courses. I've heard of the activities. I hear the major activity is avoiding work for the courses.
SUSAN. That's just plain wrong.
HOLDER. Well, well. You feel that these activities, these courses are important?
SUSAN. Yes.
HOLDER. More important than Homer?
SUSAN. Yes.
HOLDER. (*With a sigh.*) Oh dear. And you speak for the whole class?
SUSAN. Yes.
HOLDER. And so I've got to speak for Homer, don't I? (HOLDER *paces back and forth, scratching his head, thinking.*) Or rather: Homer should speak for himself. As he has for three thousand years.
SUSAN. We feel—
HOLDER. Wait, wait. I'm thinking . . . There is an incident, in Book Two, of the *Iliad,* where an insolent soldier tries to persuade the Greeks to leave Troy. The Lord Odysseus listens to the man, and then hits him over the head with a sceptre. The soldier collapses, the rebellion subsides, and everyone falls into line on behalf of the Greeks. (*He turns to her proudly.*) There it is. Right in Homer. So . . . A week from Monday, I will ask for the papers. And anyone who does not hand one in, appropriately typed, with a minimum of mis-spellings, gets hit over the head with an F. For Fail. Then you will understand Homer.
SUSAN. I think . . .
HOLDER. Write *down* what you think. About Homer. And stop playing these silly games! (*Now all business, he goes to the lectern, speaks to the audience.*) Now in the time remaining, let us consider that passage in the *Odyssey*— (*Nodding offhandedly to* SUSAN.) you may

sit down— (*To audience.*) where Odysseus lies exhausted on the beach from his struggles in the sea. . . . (*She stands there helplessly as the lights dim on them and the lectern.*)

(*Lights up on* HOLDER'S *office. The* DEAN *enters, paces, pokes through a book or two. Finally* HOLDER *comes in, sees him.*)

HOLDER. Ah. Mein Dean.

DEAN. Where the hell have you been? I've called all over campus.

HOLDER. I got the message. (*He reaches into his pocket, brings out a fistful of little pink slips which he lets flutter one by one into the wastebasket.*) See the Dean . . . Call the Dean . . . please see or call the Dean . . . (*He throws the rest away.*) You rule a paper empire, Agamemnon.

DEAN. (*Patiently.*) Where were you?

HOLDER. Jogging. I jog. In the gym. Sound mind, sound body. Every day, after class, I jog two miles around the track. It's quite invigorating now that women use the athletic facilities. But then I always take a cold shower, and read the Stoics. (*Sits down behind his desk.*) Or else see my Dean.

DEAN. Gus . . .

HOLDER. Now be calm. Their strike is broken. Strike! I abuse the dignity of American labor by terming that twitch a strike. Anyway, it's over. And Saint Joan will recant, and retire to the library to write a miserable, messy little paper.

DEAN. She's a bright girl. She did brilliantly in high school.

HOLDER. Which says all that needs to be said about American high schools.

DEAN. I'm not going to argue that, Gus.

HOLDER. I wouldn't.

DEAN. No, actually, I am the bearer of glad tidings.

THE OLD ONE-TWO

HOLDER. Ah. A raise in salary.

DEAN. No, Gus. Better. I think I can swing your sabbatical now.

HOLDER. My sabbatical!

DEAN. We found the money, Gus. I told the treasurer how long you had taught without a break.

HOLDER. I am tired . . .

DEAN. So we found the dough, Gus. You can have the second semester off. Full pay.

HOLDER. Second semester! Why I could be in Greece this spring!

DEAN. Exactly, Gus. And I think we could even cough up a little extra for transportation.

HOLDER. I could see Delphi again! We could walk among the ruins!

DEAN. Right, Gus. So shall I put you down for it, then?

HOLDER. You may put me down immediately! (*Pause.*) But what will happen here?

DEAN. Oh, well . . .

HOLDER. Who will teach the Old One-Two?

DEAN. We'll work it out.

HOLDER. Will you bring someone in? I'd want to interview him. Do you have a man in mind from my field?

DEAN. Oh we'll dig up someone.

HOLDER. Who? Name names. What have they written? It's my course.

DEAN. Well I'm thinking of opening it up a little, Gus.

HOLDER. Opening it up?

DEAN. Letting various people take a crack at various versions . . .

HOLDER. Various people, various versions! Who and what?

DEAN. We're talking about the future, Gus . . .

HOLDER. We're talking about Birnbaum, and that Russell woman, and that black man, and all those other barbarians whom you have brought into this department!

DEAN. They are fine, bright people . . .

HOLDER. You are trying to bribe me out of this place, so that those alien hordes can teach my Greeks!

DEAN. Oh Christ, Gus!

HOLDER. You *gave* them Christ! You gave them the Bible, and Dante, and Shakespeare, and they threw it all away! Very well! Now let them divide the whole modern world between them! They'll never get their hands on my Greeks!

DEAN. They are not your Greeks, Gus . . .

HOLDER. They are mine, and I'll stand and protect them like a Spartan at Thermopylae! I will not allow these people, with their beards, and their cheap careerism, and their peasant sensibilities, to get their foul, unwashed hands on my Greeks!

DEAN. Oh can it, Gus.

HOLDER. The Greeks are mine. And they stay mine. And I stay here. And I will not be lured onto the rocks by the siren song of a sabbatical spring in Greece!

DEAN. At least think of your wife!

HOLDER. My wife?

DEAN. At least discuss it with her.

HOLDER. My wife stays out of this.

DEAN. That's just it. You keep her out there in the woods. You never bring her in. I never see her at the functions.

HOLDER. Don't you dare mention my wife!

DEAN. Oh Gus . . .

HOLDER. And don't call me Gus. I'm Professor Holder to you. And I am in charge of the Greeks!

DEAN. The course is doomed.

HOLDER. Not while I'm alive. And no Dean can prevent me from teaching it.

DEAN. I'm going to try.

HOLDER. Fine. Try. Take away my classroom. I'll teach it in the halls. Take away my schedule. I'll teach it at night. Take away my students, and I'll teach it to the janitor who comes in to erase from the blackboard the presumptuous scrawls of Birnbaum, Russell, and Johnson. Now please go. I have work to do. Unlike them, I read. I study. I prepare. (*He picks up a book. The* DEAN *looks at him, then storms out angrily. After the* DEAN *has gone,* HOLDER *puts down his book and dials the telephone.*) Darling, I'll be late tonight . . . No, I've got to work . . . I want to be exceptional this term . . . I have the feeling it's crucial . . . No, I'll get a sandwich from the machines, and be home very late. I'll walk from the bus . . . Goodbye, darling. I'll miss you, as always.

(*The lights fade up on the* DEAN'S *office. The* DEAN *storms in, goes to his telephone, pushes a button.*)

DEAN. Get me Professor Holder's home, will you? . . . They live somewhere out in Arcadia . . . (*He waits, shuffling angrily through papers. The telephone buzzes. He answers.*) Hello? . . . Is this Mrs. Holder? . . . We've never met, Mrs. Holder, but I'm your husband's Dean, and I think he's making a serious mistake, and I'd like to come out and talk to you about it some time . . . Now? . . . Right now? (*Consults watch, memo calendar.*) But I've got— (*Decides.*) All right. Now. (*Grabs a pencil and pad.*) Yes . . . Beyond the church . . . Beyond the graveyard . . . Turn right at a grove of trees. Yes. Fine. Got it. I'll be there . . . Goodbye, Mrs. Holder. (*Hangs up; pushes a button; speaks into other telephone.*) Cancel all appointments for the rest of the day. (*Hangs up; gets up and grabs his coat and leaves as the light fade on his office.*)

(*The lights come up on* SUSAN GREEN'S *dormitory room. Her telephone is ringing. She comes in carrying a stack of books which she throws angrily down on her bed. She answers the telephone.*)

SUSAN. Hello? . . . No, I'm sorry, Tommy. I can't go out after all. I'm going to write the paper. I said I'm going to write it. Everyone else has chickened out, and is writing one, and I'm going to do it too . . . Oh yes I am . . . I took every book on Homer out of the library, and I'm cutting all my other classes, and I'm going to write me the best goddamn paper he ever say . . . Oh yes, footnotes, references, maps, the works! . . . And I'm going to have it typed professionally at a buck a page. . . . And I'm going to show up in class every day. And sit there with my eager little eyes on him. And nod at his sappy points. And smile at his crumby jokes. And take huge stacks of notes . . . Oh yes. And after I've handed in the paper, and he's corrected it, I'm going to put on my best little dress from Pick and Puke. And comb my hair neat as a pin. And wear lipstick. And I'm going to show up in his office, and sit there with my knees together, and listen politely while he gasses on about my good work . . . No, no, wait. And then . . . and then . . . when he hands me the paper, when he hands it back, I'm going to stand up and say, very quietly and very clearly: "This is all you want, you chickenshit bastard. A lot of old words from a lot of old books. Anyone dumb enough to take the time can write this crap. So you can take this paper, and you can shove it up your classical ass!" . . . I am, Tommy. I'm going to do it. And I'm going to tear it up and throw it in his face. He'll flunk me, but it'll be worth it. He'll learn something. So goodbye. I want to get going on this thing. (*She hangs up; gets ready to read and take notes; looks around; runs off angrily.*) Oh God! Does anybody have a pencil?

(*The lights come up on the lectern.* HOLDER *is finishing a lecture.*)

HOLDER. (*To audience.*) . . . and let me conclude the class by asking you to realize how much it means when Odysseus decides to leave his home and fight for the Greeks. Consider this line: (*He reads, translating.*) "He yearned to see the smoke from his own hearth, rising." (*He looks out, reflectively.*) Consider that. The natural

THE OLD ONE-TWO

yearning of the man, the natural rising of the smoke. Both are the same. Men yearn for their hearth just as naturally, just as inevitably, as smoke rises from it. And so when Odysseus leaves Penelope at her loom in order to do battle for the Greeks, he is willfully turning his back on the very ground of his being. And that is very difficult to do. (*The bell rings.*) Ah. The bell. (*Holds up his hands.*) One moment please. I have corrected your papers. You may retrieve them, graded and with appropriate comments, outside my office at any time this afternoon. Those papers which are unusually good, or unusually bad, I will retain and return personally during office hours. Therefore, if your paper is not in the batch outside my door, see me personally at your convenience, and at mine. (*The lights dim on the lectern as he gathers up his things and exits.*)

(*The lights come up on the* DEAN *dictating, in his office, as he paces.*)

DEAN. Dear Mrs. Holder. (*Pause.*) Just a short quick note to thank you for a most pleasant afternoon. While we barely touched on the purpose of my visit, I enjoyed immensely our stroll through the misty orchard, our chat by the fire, the cheese, the wine, the music in the background . . . (*He forgets he is dictating, continues dreamily.*) the highlights in your hair . . . your deep dark eyes . . . your throaty voice with its mysterious accent . . . (*Pause. He dreams. Then he snaps out of it. He adjusts his dictaphone and starts again.*) Dear Mrs. Holder. I have always been especially fond of Simone Signoret . . . (*Stops; starts again.*) Dear Mrs. Holder. You might think that we administrators lead shallow, rootless, abstract lives. (*Pause.*) We do. (*Pause.*) Which is why we need occasionally to drink at the well . . . lean on the breast . . . touch the source. . . . (*Pause; starts again.*) Dear Mrs. Holder. Just a quick note. Just a quick , , , Just a quickie . . . (*Pause; puts down his dictaphone; looks up a number in his rotary memorandum file, and dials impulsively.*) Hi. This is— (*Pause.*) How did you know I'd call. (*Pause; laughs.*) Yes, well, listen, I feel we barely touched—on the purpose of my visit, and I'd like to come out again. (*Pause.*) Tonight? Dinner? But I'd prefer it if he wasn't—? (*Pause.*) Dinner it is, then. I'll be there. Goodbye, Simone Signoret—I mean, Mrs. Holder. (*Hangs up dreamily, then pushes a button on his intercom.*) Call my wife. Tell her to take the kids to MacDonald's. I've got to go out of town for the evening. (*The lights dim on the* DEAN.)

(*The lights come up on* HOLDER'S *office, where* SUSAN *now sits demurely gotten up, jaw set, hair neat and tied back, hands clasped in her lap. After a moment* HOLDER *come in. He sees her.*)

HOLDER. Ah. Miss Susan Green.
SUSAN. The door was open. So I came in.
HOLDER. How well you look.
SUSAN. (*Coldly.*) Thank you.
HOLDER. You've changed a great deal.
SUSAN. I've changed my clothes.
HOLDER. They're very becoming. I am reminded of a line from the *Electra:* "I now wear different robes." (*He sits behind his desk; stares intently at her.*)
SUSAN. What about my paper?
HOLDER. Ah. Your paper.
SUSAN. It wasn't in the pile. Do you have it?
HOLDER. Of course I have it. By all means I have it. (*He continues to stare at her.*)
SUSAN. May I see it?
HOLDER. (*Snapping out of it.*) Oh of course. (*He rummages through his briefcase.*) I have it right here. (*He gets it out, holds it.*) I've read it three times. Once last night, once this morning, and once about an hour ago. (*Pause. He looks at it.*)
SUSAN. May I have it back?

HOLDER. Certainly. Here you are. (*He hands it across his desk to her.*)

SUSAN. (*Looking at the title page.*) There's no grade on this paper.

HOLDER. I know.

SUSAN. (*Flipping through it.*) No comments either . . . Nothing in the margins. (*Flips through to the end.*) Nothing at the end. Nothing. You didn't write anything.

HOLDER. I know.

SUSAN. But why? Was it that—bad?

HOLDER. No, no. It wasn't that bad. No, no.

SUSAN. That good, then? You refuse to give A's? You refuse to—

HOLDER. No, no, no. It was neither. Neither good nor bad. Those categories don't apply. May I have it again? (*Holds out his hand for it; she gives it to him; he peruses it.*) Miss Green, I have never read a paper like this in all the years I have been teaching. I couldn't grade it, I couldn't comment on it. I simply read it, and was amazed.

SUSAN. I don't understand.

HOLDER. Ah, Miss Green, now I see why you protested so violently against writing a paper. And I don't blame you! The Herculean labor that this must have entailed! Your footnotes, your references, the way you move in and out of thousands of years of scholarship! It's a staggering job, Miss Green, and frankly I'm stunned by it!

SUSAN. But then why didn't you give me an A?

HOLDER. Oh, Miss Green: because this paper is dead.

SUSAN. Dead?

HOLDER. Dead. It is finally and simply a compilation of what other people have written. You don't trust yourself. You don't trust Homer. You lean on others. And that's ultimately dull. And dead. (*Long pause.*)

SUSAN. Oh.

HOLDER. And that's why I couldn't grade your paper. I could give you an A for the most dogged kind of effort. I could give you an F for an appalling lack of insight.

But what, really, is the grade between zero and infinity? (*Pause.*) So I gave you nothing at all. (*Pause. They sit looking at each other. Then she gets up and holds out her hand.*)

SUSAN. Could I have it, please?

HOLDER. I have more to say, Miss Green.

SUSAN. Could I have my paper, please.

HOLDER. Miss Green . . .

SUSAN. I want my paper. I want it back.

HOLDER. Sit down, Miss Green. I said sit DOWN. (*She does.*) Now. (*Pause.*) Do you know why I came to America?

SUSAN. The war?

HOLDER. Wrong. I came after the war. Why did I come?

SUSAN. To be free?

HOLDER. Here? Free? No, no. A scholar has more freedom over there.

SUSAN. I don't know, then.

HOLDER. I came to America, Miss Green, because I am convinced that this country will be the new Byzantium.

SUSAN. Oh, please . . .

HOLDER. The custodian of classical culture during the Dark Ages to come.

SUSAN. Oh now, come *on* . . .

HOLDER. I believe that, Miss Green. I believe that long after Rome and Paris and Florence have smothered in their own traffic, when Venice has sunk into the sea, and the Mediterranean is a sewer, and all of Europe lies poisoned in its own garbage, I believe that America will live on to tell the tale. You will keep alive what Europe kept alive for two millenia. It's your turn now. (*He quotes.*) "Some God has led me over the wine-dark seas to build his altar on these dew-washed shores." (*Pause.*)

SUSAN. Why tell me?

HOLDER. Because you're it, Miss Green.

SUSAN. I'm what?

HOLDER. You're America! You're the future! Young,

bright, energetic, and underneath it all, like your founding fathers, abiding love for the great traditions of Greece and Rome!

SUSAN. I *don't* have an abiding love . . .

HOLDER. You do, Miss Green. This paper did not spring full-armed from the head of Zeus! You wrote it!

SUSAN. I wrote it because I was mad—

HOLDER. You wrote it because you're an American. And I am telling you this because you are everything I came to this country for. And now I want to pass on the gauntlet. Now I want to turn you into a first-rate classical scholar.

SUSAN. I'm not going to be a classical scholar.

HOLDER. You are going to be the *best,* Miss Green. I am going to teach you. I intend to plant the seeds of Greece in you, and water and train and prune you till you produce nothing but Golden Apples! And I intend to start now, Miss Green. I want you to write another paper. I'm assigning a topic: Book Six of the *Odyssey.* Write on that.

SUSAN. I won't.

HOLDER. You will. (*He hands her a book.*) Use my copy. Write something good! Turn it in soon. Come by for conferences. As for this paper, this . . . dry run . . . (*He tears it up.*) It's not worthy of you.

SUSAN. Professor Holder . . .

HOLDER. (*Grabbing his briefcase and umbrella.*) Don't talk. Stay here. Work. Use my books. Use my notes. Goodbye. I've got to leave. I'm overjoyed. I've got to jog. (*He rushes out. She rushes after him.*)

SUSAN. (*Calling.*) Professor Holder . . . Professor Holder . . . (*The lights dim on his office.*)

(*The lights come up on the* DEAN'S *office. The* DEAN *is dictating a letter.*)

DEAN. Letter to Professor Birnbaum, Miss Russell, and Mr. Johnson. Private and confidential. Dear first name. While I cannot officially promise you a renewal of contract at this time, I do feel certain that a position for you will open up in the near future. I simply don't believe that the Old One-Two will continue to monopolize our attention much longer. I fear it is an obsolete endeavor. We should no longer be tied to that tradition, or indeed any tradition. Our task today is to cultivate new life styles and new modes of behavior beyond marriage, beyond the family . . . (*Dreamily.*) beyond the church, beyond the graveyard . . . (*Pause; he snaps out of it.*) Strike that. Go back to tradition. Your course, comma first name comma, is much more appropriate for contemporary student concerns. So bear with me please. The Old One-Two is irrelevant, and I will do what I can to see that it dies a quiet, easy death. Sincerely etcetera. (*He signs off the dictaphone. Pause; then he dials his telephone.*) Hi . . . It's me again . . . (*The lights fade on the* DEAN'S *office.*)

(*The lights come up on* HOLDER *at the lectern.*)

HOLDER. Now at this point in Aeschylus, something very exciting is going on . . . (*He leaves the lectern, goes close to the edge of the stage, speaks with great excitement.*) You see, the playwright is singing a—what?—a love song, yes, a love song to the city of Athens, and to the bright new concept of human community which it represents. The Furies—those dark female forces of destruction which abide within us all—have been changed into Athenian maidens, who now carry the torches of light and understanding on into the future! And those torchbearers . . . (*He stops, peers out.*) These maidens who were once Furies . . . (*He scans the audience.*) But where is our Miss Green? (*Pause.*) I don't see Miss Green here. Is she ill? Does anyone know? (*Pause.*) I hate to continue the lecture without— (*Pause, then suddenly.*) Class dismissed. (*He gathers up his books and briefcase very quickly.*) I said, class dismissed. I was up half the night. Working this out for— (*Pause.*) Class dismissed. (*He hurries offstage.*)

THE OLD ONE-TWO

(*Lights come up on* HOLDER'S *office.* SUSAN *sits in a chair, waiting grimly. After a moment he dashes in.*)

HOLDER. Where have you been?
SUSAN. Waiting right here.
HOLDER. Why weren't you in class?
SUSAN. Because I wanted to think.
HOLDER. That's something, at least. And have you been reading?
SUSAN. Yes.
HOLDER. Have you read Aeschylus?
SUSAN. No.
HOLDER. You should have read Aeschylus.
SUSAN. (*Patting the book.*) I read this. Book Six of the *Odyssey*. I read it many times.
HOLDER. We will talk about Aeschylus. That's where **I am**.
SUSAN. No. I want to talk about this. (*She indicates the book.*) That's where *I* am. And that's where you are, too, really, I think.
HOLDER. What do you mean?
SUSAN. Professor Holder, I wonder if you realize what Book Six of the *Odyssey* is about.
HOLDER. Of course I realize. It's about—
SUSAN. It's about an older man falling in love with a younger girl, that's what it's about.
HOLDER. It's about—
SUSAN. It's about the aging Odysseus, naked and alone, exhausted from his battles for the Greeks, finding himself on a strange island, and falling in love with the young princess of that island.
HOLDER. It is not about—
SUSAN. It is about how he loves her, and forgets his home because of her.
HOLDER. It happens to be about—
SUSAN. It's about *that*, Professor Holder. I've read it very recently, and very carefully, and that's what it's

about. And I think when you assigned it to me, you knew that.

HOLDER. I did *not*—

SUSAN. *Unconsciously.* You knew that. (*Pause.*)

HOLDER. (*Very quietly.*) I think you're wrong.

SUSAN. I know I'm right. I've been working very hard. And now I know a lot of things. I know, for example, that the teaching relationship is basically erotic. I know that the hostility you felt toward me at the beginning of the term was an aspect of that eroticism. I know that your remarks about my clothes were more overt signs of it. I know your desire to jog is an attempt to sublimate it. And I know that in Book Six of the *Odyssey* you were signaling to me your erotic impulses in the only way you knew how. (*Long pause.*)

HOLDER. Birnbaum! Russell! Johnson! You've been talking to the barbarians!

SUSAN. I haven't talked to anyone. These are my own conclusions.

HOLDER. They are *stupid* conclusions! They are *insulting* conclusions. They are a ghastly example of cheap, high school, assembly-line, American-made Freud! And I refuse to discuss them.

SUSAN. (*Calmly, getting up.*) I knew you'd say that. (*She puts the book down on his desk.*) And so I'm dropping this course.

HOLDER. Dropping it?

SUSAN. Because it's a lie. I think I sensed it even in September. You refuse to deal with these things. You refuse to consider the entire world of the unconscious. (*Indicating book.*) You avoid the heart of the matter. And therefore the Old One-Two is just one long lie! (*She goes to the door.*)

HOLDER. (*Shouting.*) *We have not finished this conference!* (*Pause; she turns; he controls himself.*) In private conferences, I believe in giving students ample time to make their case. (*Pause.*) No matter how absurd the case may be. (*Pause.*) So we will discuss Book Six of the Odyssey in more detail. (*Pause.*)

Susan. O.K. (*She moves toward the chair.*)

Holder. Perhaps you'd better close the door. (*She looks at him.*) The noise from the corridor can be distracting.

Susan. All right. (*She closes the door, sits down, watches him.*)

Holder. (*Holding out the book to her.*) Would you like to refresh your memory?

Susan. No thanks. I know it cold.

Holder. All right. (*He shuffles through the papers.*)

Susan. Page 76.

Holder. Yes. Here it is. Odysseus is cast up on the shore of a strange island.

Susan. America.

Holder. America is not a strange island.

Susan. It is to you. (*Pause.*)

Holder. He is exhausted. He falls asleep.

Susan. As you did.

Holder. I did not.

Susan. Teaching the Old One-Two. Year after year. You fell asleep. (*Pause.*)

Holder. He awakens to the sound of young girls playing ball.

Susan. Playing games.

Holder. Who is playing games?

Susan. You called my strike a silly game! (*Pause.*)

Holder. (*With increasing energy.*) He watches these girls from his hiding-place.

Susan. Hiding behind his lectern.

Holder. And finally, hungry and forlorn . . .

Susan. Eager for life . . .

Holder. He approaches the lovely princess . . .

Susan. As you did me . . .

Holder. Covering his naked loins with a thick branch . . .

SUSAN. Covering your sexual desires with Book Six of the *Odyssey* . . .

HOLDER. And he introduces himself to her . . .

SUSAN. How do you do? (*Long pause.*)

HOLDER. (*Passionately.*) He never touches her!

SUSAN. Homer doesn't say.

HOLDER. Never does he touch her!

SUSAN. It's implied in every line!

HOLDER. He respects her innocence!

SUSAN. Oh she's not innocent!

HOLDER. She's a maiden!

SUSAN. Oh, Professor Holder. Don't be naive! (*Another long pause. He looks at her very carefully.*)

HOLDER. (*Slowly.*) Then you think . . . that this young princess . . . herself . . . feels . . . attracted to . . . this tired, naked, foreign old man? (*Pause.*)

SUSAN. I think she is fascinated by him. (*He closes the book. They look at each other for a long time. Finally:*)

HOLDER. Euripides.

SUSAN. What?

HOLDER. I said Euripides. It is time to teach Euripides. Not Aeschylus. He's too optimistic. Not Sophocles. He's too profound. No, it is time to teach the tragedies of Euripides!

SUSAN. Does Euripides write about—this?

HOLDER. In every word! Come to class. Please. Every day.

SUSAN. All right. I will. And I'll listen very carefully. (*She starts for the door, then stops.*) But what's his solution?

HOLDER. Solution? Euripides? Oh Susan Green, you should know: people die in Euripides. (*They look at each other as the lights dim on them.*)

(*The lights come up on the* DEAN'S *office. All his telephones are ringing. The* DEAN *comes in hurriedly, looking harrassed. He speaks to his intercom.*)

DEAN. No calls, please! Not one! Tell them I'm getting

out a memorandum . . . (*He sinks into his chair, loosens his tie, then takes his dictaphone and begins to dictate.*) Memo. From the Dean. To the University Community. Subject: The Old One-Two. (*Pause.*) One. In order to accommodate the increased attendance, Professor Holder's lectures on Euripides will henceforth take place in Gardner Auditorium. Two. Inasmuch as the Euripides lectures are now being taped for Educational Television, students are asked to restrain their cheers and applause until the end of the class period. Three. Because copies are no longer available in either the library or the local bookstores, students are requested to share Euripides with classmates and friends. Four . . . (*The telephone rings; he answers angrily.*) I said no calls, please . . . Oh . . . Put her on . . . (*Pause.*) Hi . . . I know, I'm sorry. I've been tied up night and day because of these goddam Euripides lectures . . . Dinner? No, I can't. The Ford Foundation is coming in. They want to en*dow* him, for Chrissake . . . Oh look, lady, I don't know why I hang around out there anyway. All I get is a good meal, and a goodnight kiss and then you send me home like a good little boy . . . I don't understand you, I don't understand him, I don't understand the students, and I don't understand Euripides. (SUSAN *comes in; he sees her.*) Call back when I can stay a little longer, O.K.? (*He hangs up.*) Ah. Miss Susan Green. I take it you now want to major in the Greeks like everyone else around here.

SUSAN. No.

DEAN. Then I suppose you are part of that Drama group which wants to put on a Euripides festival this spring.

SUSAN. No.

DEAN. Then what?

SUSAN. I want to transfer to another college, and I need your recommendation.

DEAN. Ah. I get it. To some place with a stronger Classics department.

SUSAN. No. To Saint Mary's in the Mountains. A small college for women. Which has no classics at all.

DEAN. But why?

SUSAN. Personal reasons.

DEAN. But Susan, I can't write a recommendation without knowing—

SUSAN. I didn't think so. Which means I'll just drop out. (*She turns to go.*)

DEAN. (*Coming to her; confidentially.*) Hey. He's a fake, isn't he? The course is a put-on. The Euripides lectures are phoney. That's why you're leaving, isn't it?

SUSAN. (*Turning at door.*) Professor Holder is a heroic man. The Old One-Two is a work of art. And I'll remember the Euripides lectures the rest of my life! (*She walks out.*)

DEAN. (*Calling after her.*) Susan— (*His telephone rings. He answers.*)

(*The lights come up on* HOLDER'S *office, who is also on the telephone.*)

HOLDER. Holder here. Have you got a pencil?

DEAN. Yes.

HOLDER. Then write these things down. Are you ready?

DEAN. Yes.

HOLDER. One, notify the Ford Foundation that the topic of my lecture tomorrow will be the *Bacchae*, by Euripides. I intend to connect it with Nixon, poverty, and the Viet Nam war.

DEAN. (*With a sigh.*) All right.

HOLDER. Two. I would like to meet them for lunch. There I will ask them to endow also a sequel to the Old One-Two. It will be called the New Three-Four. It will deal with the Judeo-Christian tradition. All undergraduates will be required to take it.

DEAN. Now wait a—

HOLDER. Three. I want Birnbaum, Russell, and Johnson fired. Immediately. To make room for three more Classicists.

DEAN. Gus—
HOLDER. Sorry, but I've got to go. The TV people want to work on my make-up. They say I'll be the Julia Child of the 70's.
DEAN. (*Frantically.*) Goddam it, Gus! I'm not just a flunky! Tell me what's going on! What is it with her?
HOLDER. Her?
DEAN. Susan Green. Why is she leaving, for Chrissake? (HOLDER *slams down the phone, dashes out of his office, as the lights fade on it.*) Gus? . . . Gus? . . . Oh Lord, now they hang up on me! I'm totally irrelevant. (*He puts down the receiver, holds his head in his hands as the lights dim on him.*)

(*The lights fade up on* SUSAN'S *room. Her bag is packed, her overcoat lies across it. She is sitting on the floor making a hitchiking sign: "Ride Wanted Anywhere." After a moment,* HOLDER *bursts in.*)

HOLDER. Why are you leaving me?
SUSAN. Because I can't stand it another day.
HOLDER. What? What can't you stand?
SUSAN. The course!
HOLDER. It's all for you!
SUSAN. That's why I can't stand it. Please: let me go! (*She grabs her bag and sign and tries to push past him.*)
HOLDER. If you go, everything goes!
SUSAN. I'm not up to it, Professor Holder. I'm not a tragic person.
HOLDER. Nor am I.
SUSAN. Oh you are. Those lectures were glorious!
HOLDER. They were lies.
SUSAN. Oh no.
HOLDER. Lies! I used Euripides to pander to you. I took one of the world's great playwrights, and I laid him out on the procrustean bed of my own private longings. I stretched him until he screamed anything I wanted. I turned the Old One-Two into a lie.
SUSAN. You said beautiful things.
HOLDER. Beautiful lies.

SUSAN. You believed them when you said them.

HOLDER. I did not. Do you know what I do after class? Do you know what I do after all that magnificent talk about fate and struggle and self-control?

SUSAN. You jog.

HOLDER. (*Shaking his head.*) I've given that up.

SUSAN. Then—what?

HOLDER. I read.

SUSAN. Read? What's wrong with that?

HOLDER. It's what I read that's wrong.

SUSAN. You mean . . . you read Book Six of the *Odyssey?*

HOLDER. No! I don't even read Greek anymore. (*Pause.*) I read Latin.

SUSAN. Latin?

HOLDER. And what Latin I read! I read Ovid's *The Art of Love*. I read scatalogical passages in Tacitus and Juvenal. I go to the rare book room in the library and sit there for hours, pouring over full-color reproductions of the pornographic paintings on the walls of Pompeii!

SUSAN. Gosh.

HOLDER. I hardly stop reading, except to eat. I hardly go home. Except to sleep. And when I sleep, I dream.

SUSAN. Do you dream in Latin?

HOLDER. I dream in bad Latin. The Latin I dream in is corrupt. The nouns decline lecherously. The verbs conjugate repulsively. And I dream of doing depraved things —with *you*. I dream of sloshing about with you, naked, in the baths of Caracalla. I dream of copulating with you in the crowded Colosseum while even the lions look on. I dream of taking you deep into the early catacombs, and there inventing with you a unique and fantastic coital position on top of a primitive altar, while Saint Paul and Saint Peter lead frantic prayers for our mutual damnation!

SUSAN. Oh wow.

HOLDER. (*Pacing; wringing his hands.*) Oh Susan, Susan, Susan Green! You have lured me out of Classical

Greece into the most degenerate period of all time. I stand before you, the true Roman, all buckled neatly into my armor, yet slavering and festering within! (*Pause; then she takes off her coat, puts down her bag and sign.*)

SUSAN. Take off your armor.

HOLDER. (*Backing away.*) I can't! I'd *explode!* Like an overripe pomegranate!

SUSAN. Stop talking.

HOLDER. I can't. If I did, I'd probably ravage you, like a Sabine!

SUSAN. (*Reaching out to him.*) Come here.

HOLDER. Don't *touch* me! (*Pause.*)

SUSAN. Oh look. You and I, we've got to get ourselves together, Professor Holder. I know someone who has a pad. We'll go there. We'll play records, and drink wine, and smoke grass, and relax. O.K.? I'll rub your back, you rub mine, and we'll loosen up. I mean, together, Professor Holder. O.K.? (*Pause.*)

HOLDER. (*Very quietly.*) Very well. I'll call my wife, and tell her I'm working on my lecture for tomorrow. I will say I'll be here all night.

SUSAN. Yes. I'll arrange for the pad. (*He starts for the door, then stops.*)

HOLDER. It won't be Euripides. It will never be Euripides again.

SUSAN. Let's just go. (*He opens the door, then stops, turns once more.*)

HOLDER. I'm in your power now. The entire Western Tradition is in your hands.

SUSAN. (*Putting a finger on his lips.*) Sssshh. No more talk. Let's. Just. Go. (*He looks at her, then exits. She follows after him as the lights fade on her room.*)

(*The lights come back up on the* DEAN's *office. He is at his desk, now in his shirt sleeves, a bottle and a glass in front of him. He is dictating into his machine, slightly drunkenly.*)

DEAN. . . . and so I hereby tender my resignation as

Dean of this department. Furthermore, I request a sabbatical leave so that I may travel and rest and come to a better understanding of myself and my world. I feel incompetent as an administrator, incoherent as an educator, and incapable as a man. (*The telephone rings; he answers sadly.*) Yes? . . . Oh hello. (*He sits up.*) When? Tonight? . . . All night? . . . Where? Out there? But what about—? . . . Ah. Working on Euripides, eh? O.K. Fair enough . . . Tonight he sleeps with the Greeks, and I sleep with you, and tomorrow's another day . . . Byebye, au revoir, and ciao . . . (*He hangs up, grabs his coat, puts the bottle in the drawer, starts out, stops, returns to dictaphone, takes out disk, crumples it up, tosses it away, and hurries out.*)

(*The lights come up on* HOLDER's *office. There is morning light. The telephone is ringing. Finally: the door bursts open.* HOLDER *comes in, his arm around* SUSAN, *laughing uproariously.*)

HOLDER. Susan, after last night, I am convinced you will bear me a child!

SUSAN. Oh please.

HOLDER. No, I am convinced. Whenever a god has slept with a nymph, there will be a child. You will bear him in some sacred grove of olives, and he will live to redeem America!

SUSAN. Your phone! It's time for your lecture!

HOLDER. Time is for slaves, Susan Green. Eternity is for you and me.

SUSAN. You're stoned out of your mind. I'll answer it. (*She does.*) Hello? (*Hands over receiver.*) Oh God. It's the Ford Foundation.

HOLDER. (*Regally.*) I will speak to the Ford Foundation.

SUSAN. (*Into telephone.*) He's here. But— (HOLDER *takes the phone with great dignity.*)

HOLDER. Yes, I have just finished preparing my lecture

... Euripides? Tragedy? Are you mad? ... I intend to lecture on comedy. I intend to lecture on Divine Aristophanes! I intend to talk about old men becoming young again! I intend to dance primitive, phallic dances! I intend to give you the Old One-Two! (*Pause; he jiggles the receiver.*) The Ford Foundation hung up on me. (*Pause; he looks at her, smiles.*) Oh well. Let's go back.

SUSAN. Back? Where?

HOLDER. (*Moving toward her.*) To that pad. To that superb Dionysiac music. To that sacred drug.

SUSAN. I don't want to go back. It's daylight now.

HOLDER. No matter. We'll drape the windows with batik. We'll eat crunchy Granola and organic raisins. We'll make bayberry candles and roll around on the waterbed, and do strange, calming Hindu exercises.

SUSAN. Enough is enough ...

HOLDER. Tomorrow we'll find a pad of our own. Where we'll rap and groove and rip things off. We'll—

SUSAN. Oh stop! Why are you always trying to make things into a tra*di*tion? (*Pause.*)

HOLDER. What do you mean?

SUSAN. That was it, last night. That was all. I'm together now. And you should be, too.

HOLDER. Together? *Together?* (*Grabbing her arms.*) Woman, you have *destroyed me!* (*He kisses her passionately. The door bursts open. The* DEAN *stands there.*)

DEAN. I thought so. (*Pause.*) Miss Green, you will call your parents immediately, and ask them to pick you up as soon as they can at your dormitory. (*Pause.*) Professor Holder, I will see you in my office when you are yourself.

HOLDER. (*Quietly.*) I'm myself.

DEAN. Then follow me. (*Pause; he looks at them both.*) I am appalled. (*He turns and exits.* SUSAN *looks at* HOLDER *and runs out.* HOLDER *stands for a moment, then squares his shoulders and goes out after the* DEAN.)

(*The lights come up on the* DEAN'S *office. After a mo-*

ment, the DEAN *comes in. He strides to his desk, pushes a button on his phone.*)

DEAN. (*Into phone.*) No calls, please. None. (*Slams down the receiver. He sits behind his desk.* HOLDER *comes in stoically.*) Close the door. (HOLDER *does; the* DEAN *indicates a chair near the desk.*) Sit there. (HOLDER *does. The* DEAN *puts the microphone of his dictaphone on the desk, facing the chair.*) I'm recording this conversation. Any objections? (HOLDER *shakes his head. The* DEAN *pushes the button on his machine.*) All right. I am asking you to resign immediately. If you do not, I will accuse you of moral turpitude in the next faculty meeting, and you will be voted out. There it is. Do you resign? (HOLDER *nods his head.*) Into the machine, please.

HOLDER. (*Very quietly.*) I resign.

DEAN. I have to bar you from teaching at any university in the United States. If you apply for a position, I will give you a negative recommendation. Do you contest this? (HOLDER *shakes his head; the* DEAN *indicates the mike.*)

HOLDER. (*Quietly.*) I don't contest it. (*The* DEAN *switches off the machine.*)

DEAN. Now. I have called a meeting of the Old One-Two for eight-thirty tonight. There I will announce your resignation, and turn the students over to Birnbaum, Russell and Johnson, whose contracts I can now renew and pay for out of your salary. (HOLDER *nods.*) I hope you will be there, for the sake of appearances. I hope you will plead exhaustion, and say goodbye to the students, and leave with dignity. May I count on you for that? (HOLDER *nods.*)

HOLDER. (*Suddenly.*) Why, why, why can you Americans get away with things, and I can't? Birnbaum assaults his classes with four-letter words. Miss Russell once bared her breast to make a point. Johnson teaches his students to riot regularly!

DEAN. It's not the same.

HOLDER. I'm different?
DEAN. You claim to be. (HOLDER *nods, starts for the door.*) Where will you go, Gus?
HOLDER. (*Stopping; pensively.*) Hmmmmmmm?
DEAN. Will you go home? To your—wife?
HOLDER. How can I go home?
DEAN. Go back to Europe, Gus. Go back there.
HOLDER. "I cannot stay in Thebes, nor return to Corinth." Sophocles. *Oedipus Rex.* (*He goes out majestically. The* DEAN *looks after him. Then he telephones quickly.*)
DEAN. (*On the telephone.*) Hi . . . It's me . . . (*He sighs.*) Well, you were right. He was with the girl last night . . . So that's that . . . No, he's not coming home. He says he can't. So there we are . . . Now. What I thought I'd do was move a few things out there. You know, pajamas, toothbrush, change of underwear—all very casual . . . Isn't that the way they do it in Europe? Isn't that the tradition? . . . Well when will you let me know? . . . Tonight? All right, let me know tonight . . . Wow, you are a mysterious woman, Simone Signoret . . .

(*The lights fade on the* DEAN'S *office, and come up on* HOLDER'S. *He enters, goes to his bookcase, looks at his books for a moment, shakes his head.* SUSAN *comes in, now dressed more formally.*)

SUSAN. Professor Holder . . . (*He turns to face her.*)
HOLDER. Ah, Miss Green. Should you be here?
SUSAN. I wanted to say goodbye.
HOLDER. Goodbye.
SUSAN. Did he fire you?
HOLDER. Of course. He had to.
SUSAN. My parents are driving up. In their Dodge Polara. I have to live at home, and get a job as a waitress at Howard Johnson's, and go out with nice boys my own age, and get married, and have babies, and die.
HOLDER. Oh dear.

SUSAN. I deserve it. I never was up to this. That first day, I should have just walked right out of class, straight home, back into middle America. (*She starts to cry.*)
HOLDER. Now, now . . .
SUSAN. It was all my fault.
HOLDER. No, no. It was the fault of all these stupid old books. Beware of Greeks, Miss Green. Don't trust anything written south of the Alps or before 1900. Caesar was right to burn the library of Alexandria, and I hope after I'm gone, our intrepid Dean will do the same with all of these!
SUSAN. Oh Professor Holder! What can I do? (*She runs from his study; the lights dim on him as he sweeps a stack of books off his desk.*)

(*The lights come up on the* DEAN *at the lectern. He addresses the audience.*)

DEAN. I regret that I must now announce the end of the Old One-Two. Professor Holder has decided, suddenly and sadly, to resign. When you students leave this room, you will now be able to take Professor Birnbaum, Mr. Johnson, or Miss Russell. But the Old One-Two is over, as of now. (*Pause; he looks off.*) Professor Holder wants to say a word of farewell. (*A moment. Then* HOLDER *comes out to the lectern. No books, no notes this time. He looks at the audience.*)
HOLDER. Goodbye. Read Beckett. He's the man to keep an eye on these days. Read Beckett. Goodbye. (*He starts off.* SUSAN *comes down the aisle, carrying an envelope.*)
SUSAN. Wait!
DEAN. Stay out of this, please.
SUSAN. (*Climbing onto the stage.*) No, wait. (*Waving the envelope.*) I have something for Professor Holder.
HOLDER. (*Ironically.*) A paper on Beckett?
SUSAN. (*Handing him the envelope.*) It's from your wife.
DEAN. (*Stepping between them.*) I think that can wait.

SUSAN. (*To* HOLDER.) I just drove out to see her. She gave me this envelope. She had it ready. Open it.

HOLDER. (*Putting it in his pocket.*) I don't open private mail in public.

DEAN. Of course you don't. (*To audience.*) Of course he doesn't.

SUSAN. She said to open it here. (HOLDER *looks at her; then opens the envelope.*)

HOLDER. Why it's . . . the birth certificate of our child.

SUSAN. Your child?

HOLDER. We had a child. We sent it to this country to be safe from the war. It was lost in a bureaucratic jungle. We never found it.

DEAN. But why would your wife . . . ?

HOLDER. I don't know. (*Pause.*)

SUSAN. She said to read it out loud. (HOLDER *looks at her, puts on his glasses, reads.*)

HOLDER. Date of birth: July 3, 1940.

DEAN. (*Ominously.*) That's when I was born.

HOLDER. Identifying marks: Large birthmark on left breast.

DEAN. (*Ripping open his shirt.*) That's *my* birthmark.

HOLDER. Sex: Male.

DEAN. (*Undoing his belt.*) That's what *I* am! Male!

HOLDER. (*Restraining him.*) Be calm, sir!

DEAN. (*Frantically.*) But I'm an adopted child! And they told me I came from foreign parents! And I've been lost in a bureaucratic jungle all my life!

HOLDER. (*Embracing him.*) Ah, my son! Come out and meet your mother!

DEAN. (*Agonizedly.*) I already have!

HOLDER. You have? And what happened?

DEAN. (*Collapsing against the lectern.*) She taught me the Old One-Two. (HOLDER *puts his arm around the* DEAN.)

HOLDER. Splendid! I, too, feel like teaching again!

DEAN. Teach Sophocles! Quickly! Before I go mad!

SUSAN. Teach Homer again! I loved Homer!

HOLDER. No. I think I'll teach Menander.

DEAN and SUSAN. Who?

HOLDER. Menander. A second-rate playwright who lived during the decline of Athens. He wrote tricky plots, which ended with the recovery of long-lost children and marriage. (*To* SUSAN.) You're not getting married, are you, Miss Green?

SUSAN. No, but this boy wants to move in with me.

HOLDER. (*Putting his arm around her.*) That's good enough. How about you, son? Are you getting married?

DEAN. (*Shakily.*) I already am.

HOLDER. (*Shaking his hand.*) Fine. Then Menander it is. He's second-rate, of course, and so he'll do perfectly for these decadent times. (*Pause; scratches his head.*) But wait. Menander always ends his plays with the freeing of slaves. (*Looks at audience.*) Slaves, you are now free to choose whatever course you want. But after what has happened . . . (*He puts his arm around the* DEAN.) I hope you will think twice before you try to avoid the Old One-Two. (HOLDER *smiles proudly at the audience, his arms around the* DEAN *and* SUSAN, *as the lights dim.*)

THE END

PROPERTY PLOT

For PROFESSOR HOLDER:
    briefcase
    umbrella
    books
    desk
    two chairs
    Greek bust
    telephone

For SUSAN GREEN:
    books
    notebook
    paper
    dorm furniture
    telephone
    suitcase
    overcoat
    sign
    envelope containing birth certificate

For DEAN:
    tape recorder or dictaphone
    push-button telephone
    desk
    chair
    second chair or couch
    flask

COSTUME PLOT

For PROFESSOR HOLDER:
    dark suit
    steel-rimmed glasses

For SUSAN GREEN:
    informal student clothes, i.e. bluejeans, loose blouse, sneakers
    more formal dress and shoes

For DEAN:
    various changes of shirt and jacket

SOUND PLOT

Four different kinds of rings for:
    the schoolbell
    the Dean's telephone
    Holder's telephone
    Susan's telephone

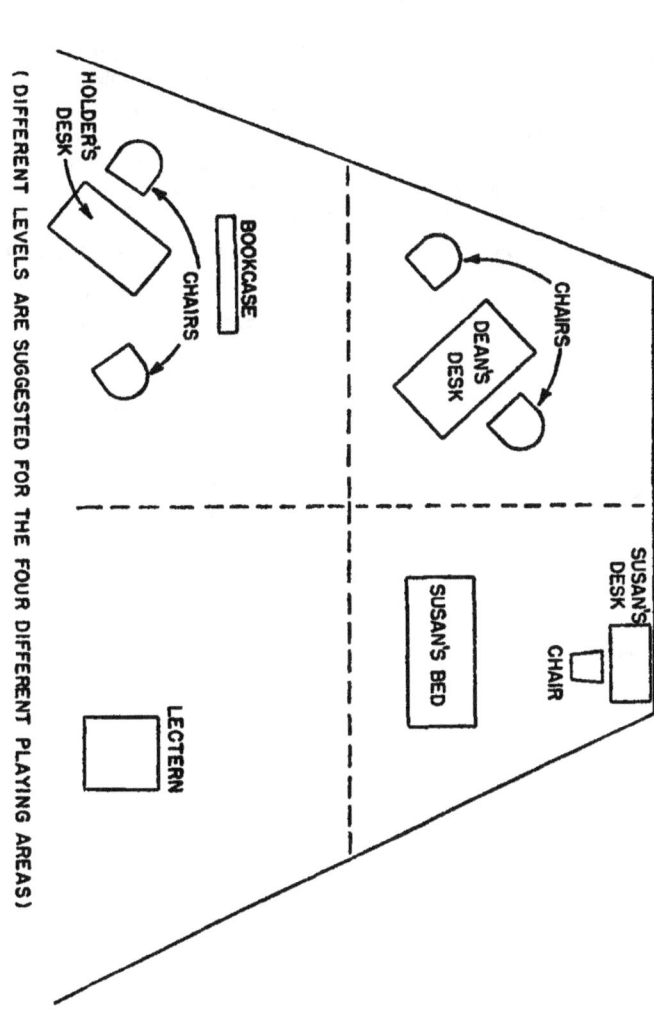
(DIFFERENT LEVELS ARE SUGGESTED FOR THE FOUR DIFFERENT PLAYING AREAS)

MUSIC USE NOTE

Licensees are solely responsible for obtaining formal written permission from copyright owners to use copyrighted music in the performance of this play and are strongly cautioned to do so. If no such permission is obtained by the licensee, then the licensee must use only original music that the licensee owns and controls. Licensees are solely responsible and liable for all music clearances and shall indemnify the copyright owners of the play(s) and their licensing agent, Samuel French, against any costs, expenses, losses and liabilities arising from the use of music by licensees. Please contact the appropriate music licensing authority in your territory for the rights to any incidental music.

IMPORTANT BILLING AND CREDIT REQUIREMENTS

If you have obtained performance rights to this title, please refer to your licensing agreement for important billing and credit requirements.

www.ingramcontent.com/pod-product-compliance
Lightning Source LLC
Chambersburg PA
CBHW072022290426
44109CB00018B/2317